ICC CRICKET WORLD CUP
ENGLAND & WALES
2019

KIDS'
HANDBOOK

Published under licence by
Carlton Books Limited
© 2019 Carlton Books Limited,
20 Mortimer Street, London W1T 3JW

ISBN 978-1-78312-453-4
9 8 7 6 5 4 3 2 1
Printed in Dubai

TM *ICC* Business Corporation FZ LLC 2018
All rights reserved

Writer: Clive Gifford
Design: RockJaw Creative
Consultant: Anthony Hobbs

The publishers would like to thank the following
sources for their kind permission to reproduce the
pictures in this book.

Cover: ALL PHOTOGRAPHY © GETTY IMAGES.
Front: (Trent Boult) Stu Forster; (Alex Hales) Clive Rose;
(Quinton de Kock) Fiona Goodall/AFP; (Virat Kohli) Paul
Ellis/AFP; (Glenn Maxwell) Mark Kolbe. Back: (Hasan Ali)
Geoff Caddick/AFP; (Thisara Perera) Robert Prezioso-IDI;
(Jason Holder) Hagen Hopkins; (Tamim Iqbal Khan) Clive
Rose; (Rashid Khan) Gareth Copley

Inside pages: ALL PHOTOGRAPHY © GETTY IMAGES:
/Daniel Berehulak: 42; /Shaun Botterill: 43; /Philip Brown:
21; /Geoff Caddick/AFP: 22; /Patrick Eagar/Popperfoto: 6-7;
/Kieran Galvin/NurPhoto: 38; /Fiona Goodall/AFP: 27; /Laurence
Griffiths: 15; /Hagen Hopkins: 25, 37; /Paul Kane: 16; /Ian Kington/
AFP: 1CR, 30T, 34; /Glyn Kirk/AFP: 29T; /Mark Kolbe: 1L, 5, 8-9, 10,
28; /Matthew Lewis-IDI: 31, 33; /Marty Melville/AFP: 11; /Indranil
Mukherjee/AFP: 9B; /David Munden/Popperfoto: 8B; /Francois
Nel-IDI: 23; /Ryan Pierse: 13, 17; /Robert Prezioso-IDI: 24, 32;
/Clive Rose: 18, 20; /Michael Steele: 1R, 14, 29B, 30B; /Harry
Trump-IDI: 19, 39; /Manan Vatsyayana/AFP: 12; /Visionhaus/
Corbis: 1CL, 35; /William West/AFP: 41

Page 36 umpire illustrations: Peter Liddiard

Every effort has been made to acknowledge correctly and contact
the source and/or copyright holder of each picture and Carlton Books
Limited apologizes for any unintentional errors or omissions that will be
corrected in future editions of this book.

A CIP catalogue record of this book is available
from the British Library.

CONTENTS

Welcome to the *ICC* Cricket World Cup 2019 4

The Home of Cricket 6

How CWC 2019 Works 8

Record Breakers! 10

Champions! 12

Great Grounds 14

MEET THE TEAMS

AFGHANISTAN 16

AUSTRALIA 17

BANGLADESH 18

ENGLAND 19

INDIA 20

NEW ZEALAND 21

PAKISTAN 22

SOUTH AFRICA 23

SRI LANKA 24

WINDIES 25

Spot the Lot! 26

Batsmen 28

Bowlers 30

All-Rounders 32

Wicket-Keepers 34

Great Match! 36

Super Skippers 38

Bat and Ball 40

Legends 42

Round Robin Matches 44

Semi-Finals 46

ICC Cricket World Cup 2019 Final 47

Answers 48

Note to readers: the facts and stats in this book are accurate as of 4 December 2018.

WELCOME TO THE *ICC* CRICKET WORLD CUP 2019

Welcome to the *ICC* Cricket World Cup 2019! This book is the perfect guide to the teams and top players, and it's packed with stats, facts, records and trivia about the ultimate One Day International cricket tournament.

What is the *ICC*?

The International Cricket Council is the organisation that runs world cricket. It was founded in 1909 and has over 100 member nations. Twelve of these play Test matches and are known as full members. The *ICC* runs competitions such as the *ICC* Champions Trophy, *ICC* T20 World Cup and the *ICC* Cricket World Cup.

What is an ODI?

The games at the *ICC* Cricket World Cup are played under One Day International (ODI) rules. Each team bats once for 50 overs or until all their players are out. The first team to bat sets a score that the second team tries to beat. Bowlers each bowl up to ten overs per game.

Where and when is it?

The 48 matches of the *ICC* Cricket World Cup 2019 will be held at 11 grounds across England and Wales. The action starts on 30 May, when England take on South Africa in what promises to be an epic contest. The games then come thick and fast throughout June, with the final to be held at Lord's on 14 July.

Left: Will the reigning champions Australia defend their title and lift the trophy for a record sixth time?

Below: The ICC Cricket World Cup trophy is 60cm high, made of silver and a thin layer of gold, and weighs 11kg – about the weight of eight cricket bats!

TROPHY TALK

Only five nations have ever won the *ICC* Cricket World Cup, but all ten sides will be battling hard at the 2019 tournament and hoping to lift the precious trophy. Can you put a tick beside all five former champions?

Answers on page 48

- Afghanistan
- Australia
- Bangladesh
- England
- India
- New Zealand
- Pakistan
- South Africa
- Sri Lanka
- Windies

THE HOME OF CRICKET

The sport of cricket was born in England hundreds of years ago. England played in the first Test match against Australia in 1877 and they also took part in the very first One Day International, also against Australia, in 1971.

Hosting History

In 1975, England hosted the very first *ICC Cricket World Cup*, when eight teams competed. England played in the first game, defeating India by 202 runs. They hosted again in 1979 and 1983, and co-hosted in 1999. 2019 is the fifth time that part or all of the tournament has been played in the home of cricket.

Lord's

Lord's *(below)* is famous as the world's oldest major cricket ground. It is the perfect venue for the final of the *ICC Cricket World Cup 2019*. So far, Lord's has hosted 54 England ODIs and it is also home to the Marylebone Cricket Club, who are in charge of the Laws of Cricket – the rules of the sport.

AROUND THE GROUNDS

The 2019 tournament will feature games played at ten different grounds in England and one in Wales. Can you match the ground name to its location on the map?

- ⬤ Bristol County Ground
- ⬤ County Ground Taunton
- ⬤ Edgbaston
- ⬤ Headingley
- ⬤ Lord's
- ⬤ Old Trafford
- ⬤ The Oval
- ⬤ The Riverside Durham
- ⬤ Hampshire Bowl
- ⬤ Cardiff Wales Stadium
- ⬤ Trent Bridge

Answers on page 48

HOW CWC 2019 WORKS

Over the years, the rules at the *ICC* Cricket World Cup have changed. At the early tournaments, for example, players wore white and each side batted for 60 overs. Today, teams wear coloured clothing and bat for 50 overs.

One big group

All ten teams at CWC 2019 will play each other once, in what is known as a round robin format. After all the group games are completed, the top four teams make it to the semi-finals.

Knockout stages

The team placed fourth after the round robin plays the top team, while the second and third teams play each other. Knockout games can be tense – if you lose, you are out! One of the closest of all took place at CWC 1999, when Australia ran out the last pair of South African batsmen with just two balls remaining *(below)*.

Above: *South Africa's JP Duminy took a hat-trick (three wickets in three balls) against Sri Lanka at CWC 2015.*

PowerPlays

ODI rules include spells of the game called PowerPlays, when a captain has to place a certain number of his fielders inside a 30-yard (27.4-metre) circle surrounding the wicket. There are three PowerPlays in an innings.

Name	When	Restriction
PowerPlay 1	Overs 1-10	Only two fielders allowed outside the 30-yard circle.
PowerPlay 2	Overs 11-40	Up to four fielders are allowed outside the 30-yard circle.
PowerPlay 3	Overs 41-50	Up to five fielders are allowed outside the 30-yard circle.

IND v ENG

ENG 338-8
OVERS 50

IND 338

ENG 338-8 | 50 | TARGET 339

It's a tie!

Most ODI matches end in a win for one team, but a handful of matches go right down to the final ball. If the scores are level, then the match is declared a tie. There have only been four ties at the *ICC* Cricket World Cup. The last one was in 2011 when England and India scored 338 runs each.

RECORD BREAKERS!

The *ICC* Cricket World Cup has thrown up some astonishing records over the years. Can you match each record to the right player?

For each record, choose from these players. Pick carefully – there are more players than records!

A Herschelle Gibbs

B Glenn McGrath

C Shoaib Akhtar

D Javed Miandad

E Kevin O'Brien

F Virat Kohli

G Chris Gayle

H Martin Guptill

I Lasith Malinga

J Eoin Morgan

Left: *Chris Gayle, Windies*

Right: Lasith Malinga, Sri Lanka

1 This player bowled the fastest ball in cricket at CWC 2003. His delivery was bowled at English batsman Nick Knight and was measured at 161.3km/h – that's FAST!

2 The highest innings in an *ICC* Cricket World Cup match was struck by this player at the 2015 tournament. He hit more sixes than fours, a record 16 in total.

3 The only bowler to take four wickets in a row with four balls was this player. He set the record at CWC 2007 against South Africa, who were 206 for 5 and needed just four runs to win!

4 At CWC 2007, this batsman became the first player in international cricket to hit six sixes in an over.

5 The fastest ever century at an *ICC* Cricket World Cup was scored by this player at the 2011 tournament against England. It took just 50 balls for him to score 100 runs.

Answers on page 48

CHAMPIONS!

The defending champions of the *ICC* Cricket World Cup are Australia, who defeated New Zealand in 2015 in front of a huge crowd of 93,013 fans. Only four other nations have also tasted glory. Here are their stories...

WINDIES

Captained by the shrewd Clive Lloyd, the Windies won the first two tournaments. Batsmen such as Viv Richards and Gordon Greenidge starred, as did bowlers like Keith Boyce and Joel Garner. After beating England by over 90 runs in 1979, they also reached the 1983 final, but lost to India.

1975   **1979**

INDIA

In 1983 India became the first Asian winners of the tournament when, led by all-rounder Kapil Dev, they defeated the Windies in the final. In the 2011 quarter-finals, Sachin Tendulkar's brilliant batting and Zaheer Khan's incredible pace bowling ended Australia's run of three CWC triumphs. India then beat Pakistan in the semi-finals and Sri Lanka in the final.

1983   **2011**

SPOT THE DIFFERENCE

Here's India winning CWC 2011. Can you spot six differences between the two pictures?

Answers on page 48

PAKISTAN

Pakistan started slowly in 1992, winning just one of their first five matches and sneaking into the semi-finals. A quickfire 60 in just 37 balls from Inzamam-ul-Haq and two wickets each for Wasim Akram and Mushtaq Ahmed saw them defeat New Zealand. The same bowlers each took three wickets in the final to record a memorable victory over England.

1992

SRI LANKA

Sri Lanka excited and entertained with free-scoring starts to their innings at CWC 1996, led by their talented opener and player of the tournament, Sanath Jayasuriya. In the final their hero was Aravinda de Silva, who took three wickets and scored 107 not out as the Sri Lankans defeated Australia.

1996

AUSTRALIA

Australia have dominated CWC since the late 1990s, with the dream team of run machine Ricky Ponting, outrageous hitter Adam Gilchrist, ace bowler Glenn McGrath and spin king Shane Warne. Those teams won three titles in a row, while their first victory in 1987 came from a side captained by the great Allan Border.

1987   **1999**   **2003**   **2007**   **2015**

Left: *Australia celebrate with the trophy in 2015 after beating New Zealand by seven wickets.*

GREAT GROUNDS

Eleven cricket grounds in England and Wales will proudly host matches at the *ICC* Cricket World Cup 2019. Some are new or have been redeveloped in recent years to give spectators brilliant views of the match action.

BRISTOL COUNTY GROUND
Location: Bristol
County team: Gloucestershire
Capacity: 17,500
CWC 2019 games: Three

This ground first opened in 1889 and was bought by legendary England cricketer WG Grace, who lived nearby. Six ODI centuries have been scored there so far, two by India's Sachin Tendulkar.

HEADINGLEY
Location: Leeds
County team: Yorkshire
Capacity: 20,000
CWC 2019 games: Four

Headingley has seen many great matches and moments of drama. Winston Davis of the Windies and Pakistan's Waqar Younis are the only bowlers to take seven wickets in an ODI innings there.

HAMPSHIRE BOWL
Location: Southampton
County team: Hampshire
Capacity: 25,000
CWC 2019 games: Five

The Hampshire Bowl is the newest of the host grounds. It was opened in 2001 and held its first ODI in 2003. New Zealand's Martin Guptill is the ODI top scorer here, hitting 189 in 2013.

Below: The highest ever ODI innings at Edgbaston was 408 for 9 by England versus New Zealand in 2015.

EDGBASTON
Location: Birmingham
County team: Warwickshire
Capacity: 25,000
CWC 2019 games: Five (including a semi-final)

Known for its passionate fans, Edgbaston was the first English ground outside of Lord's to host a major ODI final – the *ICC* Champions Trophy final in 2013.

THE OVAL
Location: London
County team: Surrey
Capacity: 25,500
CWC 2019 games: Five

Now a world-famous cricket venue in south London, the Oval was the location of the first international football match, between England and Scotland in 1870. The ground has the largest playing area of any of the CWC 2019 venues.

LORD'S
Location: London
County team: Middlesex
Capacity: 28,000
CWC 2019 games: Five (including the final)

The home of cricket is easy to identify, with its historic pavilion from the 1890s that contrasts with its futuristic media centre. Thirty ODI centuries have been scored at Lord's. The fastest was Jos Buttler's 121 from just 74 balls against Sri Lanka in 2014.

OLD TRAFFORD
Location: Manchester
County team: Lancashire
Capacity: 26,000
CWC 2019 games: Six (including a semi-final)

This much-changed ground was bombed during World War II, damaging its historic pavilion and several stands. In 2017, the Pavilion End of the ground was renamed the James Anderson End after the veteran Lancashire and England bowler.

COUNTY GROUND TAUNTON
Location: Taunton
County team: Somerset
Capacity: 12,500
CWC 2019 games: Three

The smallest CWC 2019 venue has stands named after two of its most famous players – Ian Botham and Marcus Trescothick. In 2018, Trescothick completed his 26th season playing for Somerset.

Above: The Pavilion at Old Trafford was originally built in 1895.

THE RIVERSIDE DURHAM
Location: Chester-le-Street
County team: Durham
Capacity: 17,000–20,000
CWC 2019 games: Three

The ground's first ODI was Scotland v Pakistan at CWC 1999. Only two bowlers have taken five wickets in an ODI game here – England's Graeme Swann and New Zealand's James Franklin.

CARDIFF WALES STADIUM
City: Cardiff
County team: Glamorgan
Capacity: 15,643
CWC 2019 games: Four

The ground's first ODI was a match between Australia and New Zealand at CWC 1999. In 2007, a rib taken from veteran Glamorgan cricketer Mike Powell was buried at the ground!

TRENT BRIDGE
City: Nottingham
County team: Nottinghamshire
Capacity: 17,500
CWC 2019 games: Five

This historic ground first opened in 1841. It has been the scene for many epic English performances, including England's highest ever ODI score, 481 for 6 against Australia in 2018.

DID YOU KNOW?
The matches at CWC 1996 were held in an astonishing 26 different grounds in Pakistan, India and Sri Lanka.

?

WHICH GROUND?
Which ground has hosted more *ICC* Cricket World Cup games than any other?

a) Eden Gardens, Kolkata, India ◯

b) Headingley, Leeds, England ◯

c) The Gabba, Brisbane, Australia ◯

Answers on page 48

AFGHANISTAN

First ODI: 2009 v Scotland

Highest ODI total: 338 v Ireland, 2017

Previous *ICC* Cricket World Cups: 1

Best performance: Group stage 2015

Players to watch: Rashid Khan, Mohammad Nabi, Mohammad Shahzad, Samiullah Shenwari

Afghanistan Cricket Board
ACB

Right: *Dawlat Zadran (right) took two wickets against Australia at CWC 2015.*

DID YOU KNOW?

At CWC 2015, Afghanistan dismissed both of Sri Lanka's opening batsman for golden ducks (out first ball) – the only time this has happened at the *ICC* Cricket World Cup.

As of the start of 2019, Afghanistan have a better ODI win ratio than England: true or false?

TRUE ⬤

FALSE ⬤

AUSTRALIA

First ODI: 1971 v England

Highest ODI total: 434 v South Africa, 2006

Previous *ICC* Cricket World Cups: 11

Best performance: Champions 1987, 1999, 2003, 2007, 2015

Players to watch: Glenn Maxwell, Aaron Finch, Mitchell Starc, Josh Hazlewood

CRICKET
AUSTRALIA

Rearrange these letters to get the name of an Australian spinner and batsman.

A N G O R A   H A T S

....

DID YOU KNOW?
Ricky Ponting captained more CWC matches than any other player – 29 over three tournaments.

Who was involved in Australia's largest ODI partnership of 284, versus Pakistan in 2017?

a) Travis Head ⭕

b) Aaron Finch ⭕

c) Glenn Maxwell ⭕

Answers on page 48

Right: Aaron Finch scored 135 against England at CWC 2015. He also scored 81 against India.

BANGLADESH

First ODI: 1986 v Pakistan

Highest ODI total: 329 v Pakistan, 2015

Previous *ICC* Cricket World Cups: 5

Best performance: Super 8 stage 2007; Quarter-finals 2015

Players to watch: Shakib Al Hasan, Mashrafe Mortaza, Tamim Iqbal, Mohammad Mahmudullah

Left: *Tamim Iqbal (far left) and Mushfiqur Rahim during their 166 partnership versus England at the ICC Champions Trophy 2017.*

Which Bangladesh player recorded a high strike rate of 173.91 during his innings against New Zealand at CWC 2015?

a) Sabbir Rahman ⬭

b) Mashrafe Mortaza ⬭

c) Tamim Iqbal ⬭

Answers on page 48

DID YOU KNOW?
Bangladesh defeated England in matches at both CWC 2011 and CWC 2015.

ENGLAND

First ODI: 1971 v Australia

Highest ODI total: 481 v Australia, 2018

Previous *ICC* Cricket World Cups: 11

Best performance: Runners-up 1979, 1987, 1992

Players to watch: Jonny Bairstow, Jason Roy, Jos Buttler, Joe Root, Adil Rashid

Can you unscramble the letters to get the names of two England all-rounders?

(E)(M)(A)(I)(L) (O)(N)(E)

(I) (S)(O)(C)(K) (W)(A)(S)(H)(E)(R)

....

....

?

In 2018, Eoin Morgan scored the fastest 50 by an England player, in just 21 balls. Whose record did he beat?

a) Andrew Flintoff ⬭

b) Joe Root ⬭

c) Jos Buttler ⬭

DID YOU KNOW?
In their world-record ODI score of 481 against Australia in 2018, England hit an incredible 21 sixes! Both Jonny Bairstow (139 runs) and Alex Hales (147 runs) faced just 92 balls.

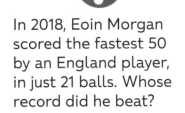

Left: *Batsman Alex Hales played two games at CWC 2015, against Bangladesh and Afghanistan.*

INDIA

First ODI: 1974 v England

Highest ODI total: 418 v Windies, 2011

Previous *ICC* Cricket World Cups: 11

Best performance: Champions 1983, 2011

Players to watch: Virat Kohli, Rohit Sharma, Shikhar Dhawan, Jasprit Bumrah, Hardik Pandya

Below: *Opening batsman Shikhar Dhawan was India's top scorer at CWC 2015.*

Which player has captained India in over 200 ODI matches?

a) Sachin Tendulkar

b) MS Dhoni

c) Virat Kohli

Answers on page 48

DID YOU KNOW?
Rohit Sharma holds the record for the highest score in an ODI. Against Sri Lanka in 2014, he struck an incredible 264 off 173 balls, including 33 fours and nine sixes.

In the very first CWC match, in 1975, India's Sunil Gavaskar scored 36. How many overs did he bat for?

a) 1   **b) 3**   **c) 11**   **d) 60**

NEW ZEALAND

First ODI: 1973 v Pakistan

Highest ODI total: 402 v Ireland, 2008

Previous *ICC* Cricket World Cups: 11

Best performance: Runners-up 2015

Players to watch: Kane Williamson, Martin Guptill, Trent Boult, Ross Taylor

GOOD MATCH

Can you match the number of sixes hit in ODIs by these three New Zealand legends?

Brendon McCullum ⭕

Nathan Astle ⭕

Stephen Fleming ⭕

a 86 **b** 63 **c** 200

?

Who has made more centuries in ODIs for New Zealand than any other player?

a) Kane Williamson ⭕

b) Ross Taylor ⭕

c) Brendon McCullum ⭕

Right: Star batsman Kane Williamson has made 44 scores of 50 or more in ODIs.

DID YOU KNOW?
Ross Taylor's full name is Luteru Ross Poutoa Lote Taylor. In 2010, he became the first player of Samoan descent to captain New Zealand.

Answers on page 48

PAKISTAN

First ODI: 1973 v New Zealand

Highest ODI total: 399 v Zimbabwe, 2018

Previous *ICC* Cricket World Cups: 11

Best performance: Champions 1992

Players to watch: Babar Azam, Mohammad Hafeez, Hasan Ali, Mohammad Amir

?

Which ex-Navy sailor hit his first ODI century when Pakistan won the *ICC* Champions Trophy 2017?

a) **Fakhar Zaman** ◯

b) **Babar Azam** ◯

c) **Faheem Ashraf** ◯

Left: Hasan Ali has taken five wickets in an ODI innings against Australia, Sri Lanka and the Windies.

Write the letter of the alphabet that comes before each one shown to reveal the name of the first Pakistan ODI player to be born in Swansea, Wales.

Ⓙ Ⓝ Ⓑ Ⓔ   Ⓧ Ⓑ Ⓣ Ⓙ Ⓝ

....

DID YOU KNOW?
All-rounder Shahid Afridi took seven wickets for 12 runs in a 2013 ODI versus the Windies. He also holds the world record for most sixes in ODIs, with 351.

SOUTH AFRICA

First ODI: 1991 v India

Highest ODI total: 439 v Windies, 2015

Previous *ICC* Cricket World Cups: 7

Best performance: Semi-finals 1992, 1999, 2007, 2015

Players to watch: Kagiso Rabada, Imran Tahir, Quinton de Kock, Faf du Plessis, Hashim Amla

Unscramble the letters to find the South African cricketer with over 5,000 ODI runs to his name.

U N P A I D
M E A N   J U L Y

....

....

DID YOU KNOW?
AB de Villiers holds all three ODI records for the fastest 50 (16 balls), 100 (31 balls) and 150 (64 balls).

Right: Batsman Aiden Markram captained South Africa to the ICC U19 Cricket World Cup title in 2014.

SRI LANKA

Sri Lanka Cricket

First ODI: 1975 v Windies

Highest ODI total: 443 v Netherlands, 2006

Previous *ICC* Cricket World Cups: 11

Best performance: Champions 1996

Players to watch: Upul Tharanga, Angelo Mathews, Kusal Mendis, Thisara Perera

DID YOU KNOW?
Sri Lankan spin bowling legend Muttiah Muralitharan has taken more ODI wickets than any other cricketer – 534, including 68 at the *ICC* Cricket World Cup.

DID YOU KNOW?
Sri Lanka bowled Zimbabwe out for 35 in 2004, the lowest ever ODI total in history.

OUTSTANDING OVER
In 2013, Thisara Perera scored 35 runs from a single over bowled by South Africa's Robin Peterson. Can you fill in the scoring chart for the over?

_ WD 6 6 6 _ 6

Left: *Hard-hitting all-rounder Thisara Perera has scored over 1,850 runs and taken more than 160 wickets in ODIs.*

WINDIES

WINDIES

First ODI: 1973 v England

Highest ODI total: 372 v Zimbabwe, 2015

Previous *ICC* Cricket World Cups: 11

Best performance: Champions 1975, 1979

Players to watch: Chris Gayle, Jason Holder, Shai Hope, Marlon Samuels

DID YOU KNOW?

Chris Gayle hit the first CWC double century (200 runs) in 2015. His 215 came off just 147 balls. His 372-run partnership with Marlon Samuels was also a record.

WHO AM I?

I am a young West Indian batsman and wicket-keeper whose older brother also played ODI cricket. In 2018, I was voted one of two male Wisden Cricketers of the Year.

Right: Jason Holder was appointed the youngest ever Windies ODI captain at 23 years and 72 days.

SPOT THE LOT!

Whether you are lucky enough to watch an *ICC* Cricket World Cup match live, or enjoy the action on TV or the internet, keep an eye out for the following moments in the games.

A century
Look out for a batsman raising his bat to the fans and team-mates after scoring 100 runs.

I spotted it!

Diving catch
Catches can win matches, so keep your eye out for any spectacular catches taken by a fielder diving or at full stretch.

Six!
If the ball has been struck and lands over the ropes or in the stands, it's a six!

Three slips
If you spot three slip fielders standing behind the batsman and in a row close to the wicket-keeper, you know the bowling team are really going on the attack!

Maiden over
Great bowling and fielding can see no runs scored off a bowler's over. Keep alert to spot one of these.

Run out
A lightning-fast and accurate throw can see the ball smash the wickets and a batsman run out.

I spotted it!

Right: *South Africa's Dale Steyn takes a full-length catch to dismiss Pakistan's Ahmad Shahzad at CWC 2015.*

Spilt chance
The ball can fly to fielders at all speeds and angles. Keep your eyes out for any catch attempts that a fielder drops.

Despairing dive
Keep your eyes peeled for a fielder desperately diving near the boundary but failing to stop a four being scored.

Colourful fans
Fans of the different nations often paint their faces in their national colours, with bright clothes and headgear to match.

DID YOU KNOW?
The Windies' Chris Gayle hit 26 sixes at CWC 2015 – a record for a single tournament.

DID YOU KNOW?
New Zealand's Trent Boult bowled a record 14 maiden overs at CWC 2015.

BATSMEN

Top ODI batsmen are run machines, able to score from almost every ball. There isn't much time to play yourself in, but these fab five know exactly when and how to attack to give their team the best chance of a big score.

GLENN MAXWELL
Country: Australia
Major clubs: Victoria, Melbourne Stars, Yorkshire, Delhi Daredevils
Born: 14 October 1988
ODI games: 87
Runs: 2,242
Centuries: 1
Half-centuries: 16

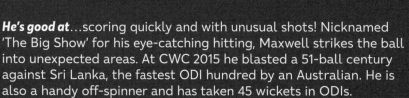

He's good at…scoring quickly and with unusual shots! Nicknamed 'The Big Show' for his eye-catching hitting, Maxwell strikes the ball into unexpected areas. At CWC 2015 he blasted a 51-ball century against Sri Lanka, the fastest ODI hundred by an Australian. He is also a handy off-spinner and has taken 45 wickets in ODIs.

MARTIN GUPTILL
Country: New Zealand
Major clubs: Auckland, Kings XI Punjab, Guyana Amazon Warriors
Born: 30 September 1986
ODI games: 159
Runs: 5,976
Centuries: 13
Half-centuries: 34

He's good at…starting an innings with a bang! This hard-hitting right-hander makes big scores with powerful drives and pull shots. He is one of only two players to have made three ODI scores of over 180. At CWC 2015 he made the competition's highest ever innings of 237 not out.

DID YOU KNOW?
Martin Guptill has only two toes on his left foot after he suffered a forklift accident when he was 13.

BABAR AZAM

Country: Pakistan
Major clubs: Zarai Taraqiati Bank Limited, Islamabad Leopards
Born: 15 October 1994
ODI games: 54
Runs: 2,267
Centuries: 8
Half-centuries: 9

He's good at…making an impact! Azam has been racking up records since his ODI debut in 2015. He is the joint second-fastest batsman to reach 1,000 ODI runs (in 21 innings) and has risen into the top ten of the *ICC* ODI batting rankings. He was Pakistan's leading ODI run scorer in 2016 and 2017.

JONNY BAIRSTOW

Country: England
Major clubs: Yorkshire
Born: 26 September 1989
ODI games: 54
Runs: 2,017
Centuries: 6
Half-centuries: 7

He's good at…thumping the ball to the boundary! A fine spell of ODI form in 2018 saw Bairstow score four centuries and a 79 in just seven innings. He has formed powerful partnerships at the top of the innings with Jason Roy and Alex Hales, but can also play in the middle order, where his fast running can turn singles into twos.

ROHIT SHARMA

Country: India
Major clubs: Mumbai, Mumbai Indians
Born: 30 April 1987
ODI games: 193
Runs: 7,454
Centuries: 21
Half-centuries: 37

He's good at…working the ball between fielders! With brilliant timing and flexible wrists and footwork, Sharma can be a nightmare to bowl at and field against. His scoring rate can explode at any moment, as shown by his 46 sixes in 21 ODI games during 2017 and a century hit in just 35 balls in a T20 game against Sri Lanka.

BOWLERS

Batsmen may get most of the glory, but great bowling can often be the difference between winning and losing. These five ODI bowlers are all potential match-winners who are set to shine at the *ICC* Cricket World Cup 2019.

KAGISO RABADA

Country: South Africa
Major clubs: Highveld Lions, Delhi Daredevils
Born: 25 May 1995
ODI games: 57
Wickets: 93
Runs: 198

He's good at…starting with a bang! An exciting, pacy bowler, Rabada announced his ODI arrival with a phenomenal performance, taking six for 16 against Bangladesh in 2015 – the best ever figures for a debut. He also played in his first Test match the same year and is already a key part of South Africa's pace attack.

TRENT BOULT

Country: New Zealand
Major clubs: Northern Districts, Delhi Daredevils
Born: 22 July 1989
ODI games: 69
Wickets: 126
Runs: 130

He's good at…taking wickets at the start of the innings! With opening partner Tim Southee, Boult swings the ball both ways and is quick, too. He was the joint leading wicket-taker at CWC 2015, with 22 wickets, five of which came for just 27 runs in a man-of-the-match performance against Australia.

MITCHELL STARC

Country: Australia
Major clubs: New South Wales, Sydney Sixers
Born: 30 January 1990
ODI games: 75
Wickets: 145
Runs: 280

He's good at…leading an attack! This tall, left-armed pace and swing bowler has taken five wickets in an innings five times and is often Australia's best ODI bowler. This was certainly the case at CWC 2015, where he took 22 wickets at an average of just 10.18 runs per wicket and was crowned Player of the Tournament.

ADIL RASHID

Country: England
Major clubs: Yorkshire
Born: 17 February 1988
ODI games: 78
Wickets: 119
Runs: 514

He's good at…breaking batting partnerships! Seemingly able to take wickets when other bowlers struggle, Rashid is an attacking leg spinner with a variety of deliveries that trouble batsmen. He has taken four or more wickets in an innings seven times and 35 of his ODI wickets have come against Australia.

RASHID KHAN

Country: Afghanistan
Major clubs: Comilla Victorians, Sunrisers Hyderabad, Adelaide Strikers
Born: 20 September 1998
ODI games: 52
Wickets: 118
Runs: 676

He's good at…taking wickets in a hurry! In 2018, Khan reached 100 ODI wickets in just 44 matches – a world record. In the same year, this tricky leg spinner became the world's youngest international captain when he skippered the ODI side against Scotland at the age of just 19.

ALL-ROUNDERS

All-rounders are an ODI team's engine room. They attack with the bat, but also work with the ball, bowling some or all of a ten-over allowance. These all-rounders are sure to entertain at CWC 2019.

ANGELO MATHEWS

Country: Sri Lanka
Major clubs: Kandy, Delhi Daredevils
Born: 2 June 1987
ODI games: 203
Runs: 5,380
Highest score: 139 not out
Wickets: 114

Sri Lanka Cricket

He's good at…batting and bowling his team out of trouble! Mathews calmly plays in the middle order for Sri Lanka, often batting with tail-enders to build a score, and bowling his accurate medium pace. He missed the final of CWC 2011 because of a leg injury, but won the *ICC* T20 World Cup three years later.

DID YOU KNOW?
In 2013, Mathews was appointed Sri Lanka's youngest ever Test captain at age 25.

BEN STOKES

Country: England
Major clubs: Durham, Rajasthan Royals
Born: 4 June 1991
ODI games: 75
Runs: 1,963
Highest score: 102 not out
Wickets: 58

ENGLAND CRICKET

He's good at…turning a game! Whether it's a spell of fast bowling, a blisteringly quick innings filled with fours and sixes, or a spectacular piece of fielding, Stokes is often at the centre of the action. He wins matches for England with the ball or bat, and in ODIs he has scored 102 and twice hit 101.

DID YOU KNOW?
Ben Stokes is a right arm medium-fast bowler but bats left-handed.

JASON HOLDER

Country: Windies
Major clubs: Barbados, Barbados Tridents
Born: 5 November 1991
ODI games: 85
Runs: 1,423
Highest score: 99 not out
Wickets: 112

WINDIES

He's good at…leading his team by example! Holder uses his 2.01-metre height to bowl tricky deliveries and strike the ball powerfully when batting. In 2017, he took five wickets for just 27 runs in an ODI win over India. The following year, he became the quickest West Indian to reach 100 wickets and 1,000 runs in ODIs.

MOHAMMAD HAFEEZ

Country: Pakistan
Major clubs: Faisalabad, Lahore Lions, Peshawar Zalmi
Born: 17 October 1980
ODI games: 203
Runs: 6,153
Highest score: 140 not out
Wickets: 137

He's good at…using all his experience! Nicknamed 'Professor', Hafeez is a solid opening batsman who has scored 11 ODI centuries. He's also a good off-spin bowler and in 2011 became the first Pakistan player (third overall) to score more than 1,000 runs and take 30 or more wickets in a calendar year.

SHAKIB AL HASAN

Country: Bangladesh
Major clubs: Khulna Division, Kolkata Knight Riders, SunRisers Hyderabad
Born: 24 March 1987
ODI games: 192
Runs: 5,482
Highest score: 134 not out
Wickets: 244

DID YOU KNOW?
Shakib Al Hasan was the first player to be top of the *ICC* All-Rounder rankings in T20s, Test cricket and ODIs all at the same time.

He's good at…turning in match-winning performances! Shakib is aggressive with both bat and ball, and he has won 18 ODI man-of-the-match awards. In 2015, he became the youngest cricketer to take 200 wickets and score 4,000 runs in ODIs.

WICKET-KEEPERS

Wicket-keepers take catches and make stumpings and run outs from behind the stumps. In a modern ODI team, they also operate as an extra batsman. They are often expected to score quickly or guide a team home at the end of the innings.

MS (MAHENDRA SINGH) DHONI

Country: India
Major clubs: Jharkhand, Chennai Super Kings
Born: 7 July 1981
ODI games: 332
Runs: 10,173
Catches: 310
Stumpings: 115

He's good at…making crucial catches and run outs as well as finishing an innings in style! Dhoni is superb at blasting quick runs to chase down a target. The veteran keeper was the first Indian batsman to score 200 ODI sixes. He has captained India at two *ICC* Cricket World Cups, winning in 2011.

TRUE OR FALSE?

1. MS Dhoni was run out for a golden duck on his ODI debut vs Bangladesh.

| True | False |

2. He has captained India to more ODI wins at home than away.

| True | False |

3. He made the highest ever ODI score by a wicket-keeper – 183 not out.

| True | False |

Answers on page 48

QUINTON DE KOCK

SOUTH AFRICA
CRICKET

Country: South Africa
Major clubs: Titans, Mumbai Indians
Born: 17 December 1992
ODI games: 98
Runs: 4,133
Catches: 139
Stumpings: 7

He's good at…getting an innings off to a good start! De Kock was a teenage baseball player and his fearless striking of a cricket ball has already seen him score 13 ODI centuries, including three in a row against India. He is also known for making spectacular catches behind the stumps.

JOS BUTTLER

ENGLAND
CRICKET

Country: England
Major clubs: Lancashire, Somerset
Born: 8 September 1990
ODI games: 122
Runs: 3,176
Catches: 153
Stumpings: 25

He's good at…smashing the ball over the boundary! Buttler is an improving wicket-keeper and one of the hardest and quickest hitters in the world. He notched up England's fastest ODI century in 46 balls versus Pakistan in 2015. Jos averages nearly 40 runs each time he bats and has blasted more than 90 ODI sixes and over 270 fours.

SHAI HOPE

WINDIES

Country: Windies
Major clubs: Barbados
Born: 10 November 1993
ODI games: 41
Runs: 1,365
Catches: 35
Stumpings: 8

He's good at…scoring runs in style! This young batsman has had some important innings, including a century in his second match. Hope averages around 40 runs every time he bats in ODIs. In 2017, he showed his skill in Test cricket, too, with a century in each innings against England.

GREAT MATCH!

The two umpires and other officials play their part by ensuring the teams play fairly and by the rules. They have to make judgements at crucial moments and can help turn a game of cricket into a great match.

NO BALL   SIX

OUT   FOUR

FREE HIT   WIDE

Signal success

Umpires communicate their decisions to the scorer and fans using a series of signals. Can you match each of the umpire's decisions on the right to the correct signal below?

....

WHICH UMPIRE?

? Below are four Elite Panel umpires, who judge Test matches and ODIs. Can you match each one to the correct fact?

⬤ ...... Kumar Dharmasena   ⬤ ...... Marais Erasmus   ⬤ ...... Ian Gould   ⬤ ...... Paul Reiffel

A) This ex-bowler won CWC 1999 with his team and took a wicket in the final.

B) This off-spin bowler played in 141 ODIs and was also an *ICC Cricket World Cup* winner in the 1990s.

C) This former professional cricketer became the first South African to win the *ICC*'s Umpire of the Year award in 2016. He repeated the feat in 2017.

D) This former goalkeeper with Arsenal was a wicket-keeper and batsman in England's CWC 1983 squad.

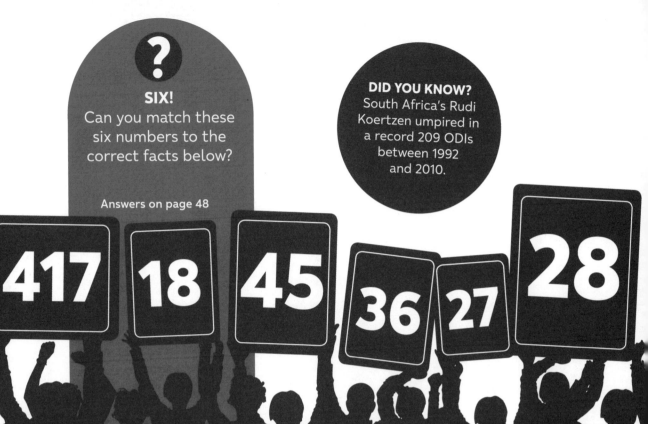

SIX!

?

Can you match these six numbers to the correct facts below?

Answers on page 48

Answers on page 48

DID YOU KNOW?
South Africa's Rudi Koertzen umpired in a record 209 ODIs between 1992 and 2010.

417 **18** **45** **36** **27** **28**

Below: New Zealand spinner Daniel Vettori appeals to umpire Johan Cloete during CWC 2015.

VETTORI 11

.... The lowest score made by a team at the *ICC* Cricket World Cup (*Canada v Sri Lanka, 2003*)

.... Number of balls needed to score the fastest half-century at the CWC (*Brendon McCullum*)

.... The record number of *ICC* Cricket World Cup matches umpired by one umpire (*David Shepherd*)

.... The highest score ever made by one team at the CWC (*Australia v Afghanistan, 2015*)

.... The most *ICC* Cricket World Cup matches won in a row (*Australia, 1999–2011*)

.... The most catches taken by a fielder in CWC games (*Ricky Ponting*)

SUPER SKIPPERS

A captain is usually one of his side's most talented players. He decides the bowling order, arranges the fielders and uses tactics to try to win the game. Look out for these four phenomenal captains at the *ICC Cricket World Cup 2019*.

KANE WILLIAMSON
Born: 8 August 1990
Country: New Zealand

One of the most talented batsmen in world cricket, Williamson was only 25 when he was made captain of New Zealand in Tests, T20s and ODIs. He has proved to be a calm and skilful leader and is hoping to add to his tally of 11 centuries and 33 scores of over 50 in ODIs.

VIRAT KOHLI
Born: 5 November 1988
Country: India

An absolute run machine in all forms of cricket, Kohli has already passed 10,000 ODI runs, including 38 centuries. At just 30 years of age, he is hungry for more. As a captain, he leads aggressively, becoming the fastest ODI captain to reach 1,000 runs and the fastest ODI player to reach 8,000 and 9,000 runs.

DID YOU KNOW?
Only two of Virat Kohli's 38 innings of 100 runs or more have ended with him being bowled out.

FAF DU PLESSIS

Born: 13 July 1984
Country: South Africa

A bold batsman who has scored over 4,500 ODI runs, du Plessis became South Africa's captain in 2017. He holds the record for the most innings (108) in international cricket without being out for a duck (no runs). At CWC 2015, du Plessis averaged over 63 runs each time he batted.

EOIN MORGAN

Born: 10 September 1986
Country: England

A former player for Ireland, Morgan has transformed the England team into an attacking side since taking charge as captain in 2015. Morgan is clever and fearless, and leads from the front with a wide range of shots, many of them unusual. He is England's leading ODI run-scorer with over 6,500 runs.

?

SETTING THE FIELD

A captain arranges his team-mates into fielding positions to stop runs being scored and take wickets from catches and run outs. This is called setting the field. Can you set this field by placing the last six fielders into the correct positions?

1 **Square leg**
2 **Long on**
3 **Leg slip**
4 **Point**
5 **Third man**
6 **Fine leg**

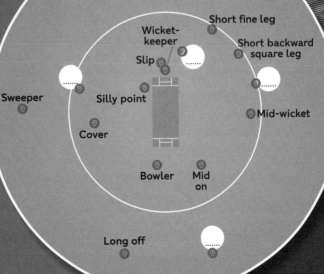

Answers on page 48

3

BAT AND BALL

Cricket is an epic contest between bat and ball, and to win the *ICC* Cricket World Cup, teams will need to perform at their peak. Can you play at your best to complete these puzzles?

SPINNER ○

UMPIRE ○

BOUNCER ○

PADS ○

WICKET ○

CATCH ○

SWEEP ○

HOOK ○

DRIVE ○

CENTURY ○

GLOVES ○

BOWLER ○

SWING ○

RUN ○

ICC CRICKET WORLD CUP WORD SEARCH

Can you find all 14 cricketing terms hidden on this bat?

```
Q F N Q I T K X S H
Y W H P E O Y W K G
A Y W K O U E S X B
S Z C H K E P S K S
B I A G P I Q U A D
W R E C N U O B D A
Q X F N X I I C K P
M I E B W I W I O X
Y R U N W D D S M K
X R B H F T S X B S
Z D U P P B X N M O
E A O T H P P W N O
R G U J N N A O B Q
I G L O V E S F P M
P E P U X A C Z G D
M B P R D V T S T B
U B O W A E K G B U
P W D W G M P S C H
O A X Y L J L M B C
X P A S H E K U Z A
C N Y E U Y R P V T
E V I R D J X C P C
K Y S P E N J U G H
J T Y A Q R M T U P
```

Answers on page 48

SPOT THE BALL

? New Zealand's Grant Elliott plays a shot in the CWC 2015 final versus Australia, but where is the ball – A, B, C or D?

DID YOU KNOW?

The world's biggest cricket bat was displayed outside the *ICC* Academy in Dubai in 2015 to celebrate the *ICC* Cricket World Cup. It was 32 metres long, 4 metres wide and weighed 950 kilograms!

MISSING NUMBERS

Write in the missing number on each cricket ball to answer the following puzzlers.

1. The most runs scored by both teams added together in an *ICC* Cricket World Cup match.   ◯ 88

2. The year Indian legend Sachin Tendulkar first played at the *ICC* Cricket World Cup.   19 ◯ ◯

3. The number of countries which hosted games during the *ICC* Cricket World Cup 1999.   ◯

4. The record number of runs made by Sri Lanka's opening batsmen, Upal Tharanga and TM Dilshan, in a match at CWC 2011.   2 ◯ 2

5. The number of overs it took Canada to score 45 in their innings against England at CWC 1979.   ◯ 0.3

LEGENDS

Many players leave their mark on the *ICC* Cricket World Cup for their enduring and brilliant performances. Here are four true legends of the game who have shined at the tournament.

WINDIES

VIV RICHARDS

Born: 7 March 1952
Country: Windies
ODI runs: 6,721
ODI wickets: 118

The 'Master Blaster' was a brilliant batsman and off-spin bowler. Richards was the first player to reach 1,000 ODI runs and 100 wickets, and he won two *ICC* Cricket World Cups with the Windies and 31 ODI man-of-the-match awards. His 1984 innings of 189 not out against England is considered one of the greatest ODI innings of all time.

SACHIN TENDULKAR

Born: 24 April 1973
Country: India
ODI runs: 18,426
ODI wickets: 154

The 'Little Master' was India's finest ever batsman and a record 2,278 of his ODI runs were scored at the *ICC* Cricket World Cup. He was awarded Player of the Tournament in 2003 and was part of the winning India side in 2011. He also holds the records for most centuries (6) and half-centuries (21) at the competition.

CRICKET
AUSTRALIA

GLENN MCGRATH

Born: 9 February 1970
Country: Australia
ODI runs: 115
ODI wickets: 381

Nobody has taken as many wickets at the *ICC* Cricket World Cup (71) as Glenn McGrath. A three-time CWC winner with Australia, he also recorded the best ever bowling figures in the competition when he took seven wickets for just 15 runs in 2003. He was Player of the Tournament in 2007 when he took 26 wickets – another record.

IMRAN KHAN

Born: 5 October 1952
Country: Pakistan
ODI runs: 3,709
ODI wickets: 182

A dangerous fast bowler and brilliant attacking batsman, Khan played his first ODI game in 1974. An amazing 18 years later, he led Pakistan to the final of *ICC* Cricket World Cup 1992, where he made the highest score of either side (72) and took the very last wicket of the game to help record a memorable victory.

DID YOU KNOW?
Glenn McGrath took a wicket with his very last ball in Test cricket and his second-from-last ball in ODIs at CWC 2007.

ROUND ROBIN MATCHES

Check out all the group-stage games at CWC 2019. Write in the winners of each match or 'tie' if the game ends up tied.

30 May	England v South Africa, *The Oval*	
31 May	Windies v Pakistan, *Trent Bridge*	
1 June	New Zealand v Sri Lanka, *Cardiff Wales Stadium*	
1 June	Afghanistan v Australia, *Bristol County Ground*	
2 June	South Africa v Bangladesh, *The Oval*	
3 June	England v Pakistan, *Trent Bridge*	
4 June	Afghanistan v Sri Lanka, *Cardiff Wales Stadium*	
5 June	South Africa v India, *Hampshire Bowl*	
5 June	Bangladesh v New Zealand, *The Oval*	
6 June	Australia v Windies, *Trent Bridge*	
7 June	Pakistan v Sri Lanka, *Bristol County Ground*	
8 June	England v Bangladesh, *Cardiff Wales Stadium*	
8 June	Afghanistan v New Zealand, *County Ground Taunton*	
9 June	India v Australia, *The Oval*	
10 June	South Africa v Windies, *Hampshire Bowl*	
11 June	Bangladesh v Sri Lanka, *Bristol County Ground*	
12 June	Australia v Pakistan, *County Ground Taunton*	
13 June	India v New Zealand, *Trent Bridge*	
14 June	England v Windies, *Hampshire Bowl*	

15 June	Sri Lanka v Australia, *The Oval*	
15 June	South Africa v Afghanistan, *Cardiff Wales Stadium*	
16 June	India v Pakistan, *Old Trafford*	
17 June	Windies v Bangladesh, *County Ground Taunton*	
18 June	England v Afghanistan, *Old Trafford*	
19 June	New Zealand v South Africa, *Edgbaston*	
20 June	Australia v Bangladesh, *Trent Bridge*	
21 June	England v Sri Lanka, *Headingley*	
22 June	India v Afghanistan, *Hampshire Bowl*	
22 June	Windies v New Zealand, *Old Trafford*	
23 June	Pakistan v South Africa, *Lord's*	
24 June	Bangladesh v Afghanistan, *Hampshire Bowl*	
25 June	England v Australia, *Lord's*	
26 June	New Zealand v Pakistan, *Edgbaston*	
27 June	Windies v India, *Old Trafford*	
28 June	Sri Lanka v South Africa, *The Riverside Durham*	
29 June	Pakistan v Afghanistan, *Headingley*	
29 June	New Zealand v Australia, *Lord's*	
30 June	England v India, *Edgbaston*	
1 July	Sri Lanka v Windies, *The Riverside Durham*	
2 July	Bangladesh v India, *Edgbaston*	
3 July	England v New Zealand, *The Riverside Durham*	
4 July	Afghanistan v Windies, *Headingley*	
5 July	Pakistan v Bangladesh, *Lord's*	
6 July	Sri Lanka v India, *Headingley*	
6 July	Australia v South Africa, *Old Trafford*	

SEMI-FINALS

The top four teams after the round robin play the semi-finals. The pressure will be on as just one more victory will take a team to the final. Use the panels below to write in the teams and match details.

9 July, OLD TRAFFORD

1ST PLACED TEAM:	4TH PLACED TEAM:
SCORE: FOR:	SCORE: FOR:
OVERS BATTED:	OVERS BATTED:
TOP SCORER 1:	TOP SCORER 1:
2:	2:
3:	3:
BEST BOWLING 1:	BEST BOWLING 1:
2:	2:

11 July, EDGBASTON

2ND PLACED TEAM:	3RD PLACED TEAM:
SCORE: FOR:	SCORE: FOR:
OVERS BATTED:	OVERS BATTED:
TOP SCORER 1:	TOP SCORER 1:
2:	2:
3:	3:
BEST BOWLING 1:	BEST BOWLING 1:
2:	2:

ICC CRICKET WORLD CUP 2019 FINAL

Fill in the details of the two teams who contest the final. Don't forget to add '(C)' beside each captain and '(WK)' beside each wicket-keeper.

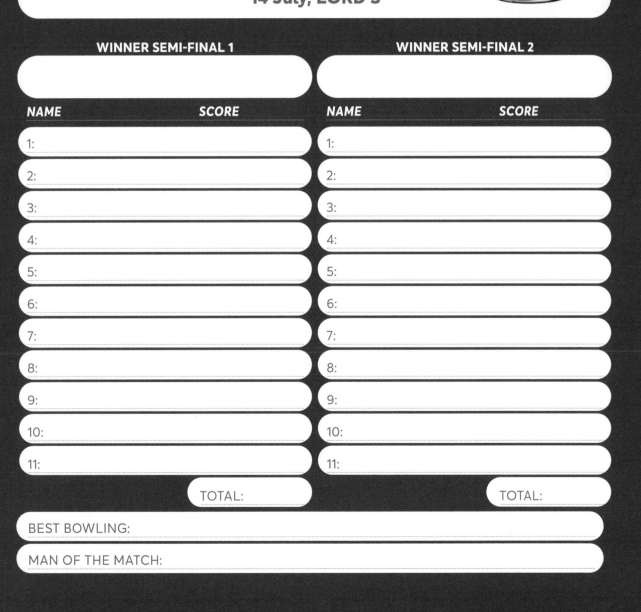

14 July, LORD'S

WINNER SEMI-FINAL 1		WINNER SEMI-FINAL 2	
NAME	**SCORE**	**NAME**	**SCORE**
1:		1:	
2:		2:	
3:		3:	
4:		4:	
5:		5:	
6:		6:	
7:		7:	
8:		8:	
9:		9:	
10:		10:	
11:		11:	
	TOTAL:		TOTAL:

BEST BOWLING:

MAN OF THE MATCH:

ANSWERS

27 – the most CWC matches won in a row (*Australia, 1999-2011*)
28 – the most catches taken by a fielder in CWC games (*Ricky Ponting*)

Page 5 Trophy talk
Australia, India, Pakistan, Sri Lanka, Windies

Page 7 Around the grounds
1. The Riverside Durham; 2. Headingley; 3. Old Trafford; 4. Trent Bridge; 5. Edgbaston; 6. Cardiff Wales Stadium; 7. Bristol County Ground; 8. County Ground Taunton; 9. Hampshire Bowl; 10. Lord's. 11. The Oval

Pages 10-11 Record breakers!
1c: Shoaib Akhtar; 2g: Chris Gayle; 3i: Lasith Malinga; 4a: Herschelle Gibbs; 5e: Kevin O'Brien

Page 12 Spot the difference

Page 15 Which ground?
b) Headingley, Leeds, England

Page 16 Afghanistan
True

Page 17 Australia
Anagram: Ashton Agar
a) Travis Head

Page 18 Bangladesh
a) Sabbir Rahman

Page 19 England
Anagrams: Moeen Ali, Chris Woakes
c) Jos Buttler

Page 20 India
b) MS Dhoni
d) 60 overs

Page 21 New Zealand
Good match: Brendon McCullum – c: 200; Nathan Astle – a: 86; Stephen Fleming – b: 63
b) Ross Taylor

Page 22 Pakistan
a) Fakhar Zaman
Imad Wasim

Page 23 South Africa
Jean-Paul Duminy

Page 24 Sri Lanka
Outstanding over: 6 and 4 (6, Wide, 6, 6, 6, 4, 6)

Page 25 Windies
Who Am I?: Shai Hope

Page 34 True or false?
1. True; 2. False; 3. True

Page 35 Anagram
Zimbabwe

Page 36 Signal success

Six   Four   Out

Wide   No ball   Free hit

Page 36 Which umpire?
a) Paul Reiffel; b) Kumar Dharmasena; c) Marais Erasmus; d) Ian Gould

Page 37 Six!
36 – the lowest score made by a team at the *ICC* Cricket World Cup (*Canada v Sri Lanka, 2003*)
18 – number of balls needed to score the fastest half-century at the CWC (*Brendon McCullum*)
45 – the record number of *ICC* Cricket World Cup matches umpired by one umpire (*David Shepherd*)
417 – the highest score ever made by one team at the CWC (*Australia v Afghanistan, 2015*)

Page 39 Setting the field

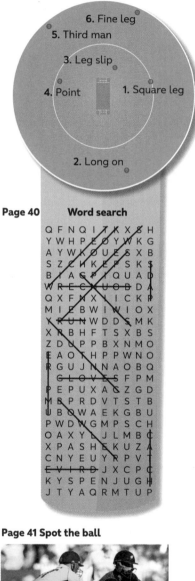

6. Fine leg
5. Third man
3. Leg slip
4. Point   1. Square leg
2. Long on

Page 40 Word search

```
Q F N Q I T K X S H
Y W H P E O Y W K G
A Y W K O U E S X B
S Z C H K E P S K S
B I A G P I Q U A D
W R E C K U O B D A
Q X F N X I I C K P
M I E B W I W I O X
X R U N W D D S M K
X R B H F T S X B S
Z D U P P B X N M O
E A O T H P P W N O
R G U J N N A O B Q
I G L O V E S F P M
P E P U X A G Z G D
M B P R D V T S T B
U B O W A E K G B U
P W D W G M P S C H
O A X Y L J L M B C
X P A S H E K U Z A
C N Y E U Y R P V T
E V I R D J X C P C
K Y S P E N J U G H
J T Y A Q R M T U P
```

Page 41 Spot the ball

Page 41 Missing numbers
1. 688; 2. 1992; 3. 5; 5. 282; 6. 40.3